the Road Back

the Road Back
The Cincinnati Bengals

photography by Thomas E. Witte
text by Lonnie Wheeler

ORANGE FRAZER PRESS
Wilmington, Ohio

ISBN 1-933197-14-5

Additional copies of *The Road Back: The Cincinnati Bengals* may be ordered directly from:

Orange Frazer Press
P.O. Box 214
Wilmington, OH 45177

Telephone 1.800.852.9332 for price and shipping information.
Website: www.orangefrazer.com

Library of Congress Cataloging-in-Publication Data

Wheeler, Lonnie.
    The road back : the Cincinnati Bengals / text by Lonnie Wheeler ; photography by
Thomas E. Witte.
        p. cm.
    ISBN 1-933197-14-5 (alk. paper)
    1. Cincinnati Bengals (Football team)--Pictorial works. I. Witte, Thomas E., 1976- II.
Title.

    GV956.C54W44 2006
    796.332'640977178--dc22

                                                            2006048310

*cover design and art direction*Jeff Fulwiler
*book design*Chad DeBoard and John Baskin

Printed in Canada

This book is dedicated to the fans. You waited fifteen years. You knew our day was coming.
You sat in the blazing heat and the blistering cold. Through rain, snow, and almost two generations
of the seventeen-year cicada, you kept rooting. WHO DEY!

Special thanks to all the Wittes, Sara Ingham, Ginna Gauntner and John Ryan who continue
to root me on. Bill Frakes for constantly pushing me to try harder and never passing up an
opportunity to tease me. Sean Meyers, Dan Powers, Mark Bealer, Bill Lackey, Terry Eiler, and Scott Gardner
for giving me a solid foundation photographically and not laughing terribly hard when I decided to freelance.
Jimmy Colton and Maureen Cavanagh for outstanding advice and demanding perfection.
Erin Gibson, Tyler Barrick, Eric Wright, Kelli Hannah, Stacy Luckey, Kate Schneider, Barbara Perenic,
Chris Doane, Jeff Swinger, Dave Kohl, Michael Keating, Ernie Coleman, Michael King, Grover Sanschagrin,
Jason Burfield, Heather Stone, and Stephenie Steitzer for allowing me to rant
(or in most cases encouraging me to rant for their own amusement).
The folks at Kidd Coffee for their Highlander Grogg and for allowing me to practically
move into their store while editing.
To those who said I couldn't do, a special thank you.

introduction

OUTSIDE THE FAMILY CIRCLE, nobody really knows what it was that finally persuaded Mike Brown to abandon his inherited customs, yank off his leather helmet, and permit his football team to be guided by another man's hand. It could have been the dozen years of wretched, relentless losing. It could have been the laughter that met the mere mention of his Cincinnati Bengals, and the institutional bungling of the name that his famous father, Paul, had personally selected. It could have been the advancing years of a man approaching 70, with children getting ever-readier to assume their birthrights in the ancestral business. It could have been the unremitting assaults rushing at him from wherever he looked or listened, and some places, such as *mikebrownsucks.com*, where he didn't. It could have been the county lawsuit that impugned the organization's sincerity and formalized the community's deep-seated dissatisfaction with it. It could have simply been the absurdity into which the situation devolved in 2002, the most pathetic of all the seasons.

That was the year that began with the Bengals being penalized for delay of game on the first play of the season; that found Corey Dillon, running the ball to the goal line for a final-seconds victory, tripping over his own lineman; that featured quarterback Gus Frerotte, under customary duress and with his throwing arm indisposed, attempting a left-handed pass, with predictable results; that saw a journeyman named Elvis Grbac, upon being offered a free-agent contract by Cincinnati, take stock and retire; that ended with a rock-bottom record of 2-14. It was the year that Brown, having had enough, fired Dick LeBeau, his gentleman coach.

LeBeau, of course, had been no worse than Bruce Coslet before him, who had been no worse than Dave Shula before him. It's hard to say when the Bengals actually secured their status as the lowliest professional franchise in American sport. The steady plummet had begun in 1991, coincidentally or not the year that Paul Brown passed on. It continued, unabated and perhaps even deepening, until Mike Brown hired Marvin Lewis in January, 2003.

There might have been other candidates that Brown at first preferred. Tom Coughlin, a hard-line veteran, would have been a hire in the old Forrest Gregg tradition, but Coughlin was unwilling to come unless the Bengals doubled their staff and entrusted him with executive authority. Mike Mularkey, a creative offensive coordinator, would have been in the Sam Wyche mold. Gregg and Wyche both took Cincinnati to Super Bowls in the 1980s. For perhaps the first time, however, the Bengals, in the act of changing coaches, turned away from their own tradition.

As a defensive coordinator for the Baltimore Ravens when their defense—the best ever, some said—won them a Super Bowl, and then for the Washington Redskins, Lewis had been rumored for numerous head-coaching jobs in the NFL. None had fallen his way. Three weeks earlier, he had declined an offer from Michigan State University. He couldn't afford to let another pass by—and certainly not a proposition of the sort that Brown, untrue to form, tendered him.

Bengals skeptics, whose ranks included the vast majority of their followers, weren't sure what to make of the mutual understanding that Brown and Lewis revealed at the new coach's introductory press conference. As the team's president, policymaker and spokesman, Brown assumed the podium only long enough to make his announcement, declining further comment and letting it be known that he would have nothing to add for the foreseeable future. If it concerned the Bengals, he said, the man to see was Marvin Lewis.

And Lewis, in turn, said this:

"I have the ability to direct the program, okay? I don't know that anybody else has stood here and told you that. I have the ability to shape and mold everything we do."

Thus began the road back.

EVEN ON THE WORST OF NFL TEAMS, good players are scattered about. Among those whom Lewis inherited, the two generally considered to be the most indispensable on the offense and defense, respectively—Dillon and linebacker Takeo Spikes—were gone within a year.

They were non-subscribers to the new order that Lewis insisted upon. Spikes, reluctant to believe that anything would truly change in the organization that he knew too well, decided before the 2003 season to exercise his contractual right of free agency. Brown's instinct, as a lawyer and progeny of Paul Brown, would have been to press his procedural advantages and thwart the player's departure; or, at least, make it as difficult as

the league allowed. Lewis's was to let the guy go. He could deal only in unanimity. And—the first confirmation, perhaps, that times had truly changed down at Paul Brown Stadium, just as advertised—it was his call.

After a year of uncomfortable coexistence, Dillon was traded for essentially the same reason. Testing Lewis in a way that wasn't wise—or maybe it was, if the objective involved getting out of town—he had set the tone for their intriguing relationship by electing not to attend the team's first voluntary mini-camp in April, 2003, suggesting that the Bengals and over-interested journalists look up "voluntary" in the dictionary. Lewis, however, had his own definition, of which the surly, record-setting running back (he had broken the NFL single-game rushing standards for rookies, first, and then for everybody) was soon apprised.

The second mini-camp was held shortly thereafter, with Dillon present and quite accounted for. Moments after the initial morning session, Two-Eight, as he liked to call himself, was scheduled to address the media for the purpose of showing contrition over his previous indiscretion. As the appointed time arrived, Lewis stood in a corner of the Bengals' locker room, arms folded, eyes narrowed. The instant the clock clicked off the predetermined minute, the coach strode meaningfully into the training room, where players often hide out to avoid reporters. Seconds later, Dillon—who had once, during a contract dispute, declared that he would rather flip burgers than continue on with the Bengals—was at his podium in full humility mode, with Lewis leaning conspicuously against a wall.

"My man," said Dillon, nodding at his all-business boss. "That's my guy."

It was the first direct challenge of Lewis's administration, and well-met. Against that background, Dillon served out a sputtering season that found him injured from time to time, raising an opportunity for his quiet backup, Rudi Johnson. Producing in unexpected totals, and without complaint or calling attention to himself, Johnson soon became a fan and staff favorite. Dillon, in turn, soon became dispensable. After all the games were played, he was dispatched to New England—where he contributed heavily to a Super Bowl championship—for a second-round draft choice.

The shucking of stars was not essential to Lewis's grand scheme, but neither was it agonizing to the exacting head coach. His charge was to establish a fresh culture within the Cincinnati franchise, and that entailed new players in significant quantity. Lewis had said, straightaway, that his first order of business was to evaluate every member of the failing team—"the process that hasn't been taking place"—and, sure enough, by the time the 2003 season was under way, the Bengals' roster included two dozen men who hadn't been on it in 2002.

Among those were several free-agent signings that had been more prompt than spectacular, which, given the Bengal precedents, was a fine start. By satisfying his most urgent needs with available veterans, Lewis was then free to spend the league's first draft choice on a player not required to pan out immediately. He was able to take Carson Palmer.

Palmer's selection was a sanguine blend of tradition and transition. The Bengals had always been known as a quarterback-centered organization. Paul and Mike Brown had both played the position themselves, and PB, furthermore, had unforgettably seen, back with his original Browns, what a guy like Otto Graham could mean to a program. In turn, Cincinnati's best years had revolved around Ken Anderson and Boomer Esiason. More recently,

though, the pre-Lewis struggles had featured, under center, the likes of Aliki Smith, Gus Frerotte, Jeff Blake, Neil O'Donnell, Paul Justin, Donald Hollas, and David Klingler.

The debacle of 2002 had begun with an abominable three-deep quarterback derby, the candidates being Frerotte, Smith, and Jon Kitna. Frerotte was the man until he waxed ambidextrous, whereupon Kitna became an able caretaker. Kitna's welcomed competence was another reason that Palmer, the shiny Heisman Trophy winner from Southern California, could be skimmed from the top—the Bengals actually signed him two days in advance of the draft—and brought along deliberately.

The rich rookie wouldn't play a play in 2003. The games, it turned out, mattered too much.

As the longsuffering Cincinnati football fans, back from their estrangement on the promise of a page turned, poured into Paul Brown Stadium for the 2003 season opener, the Sting song, *Brand New Day*, pelted them from the loudspeakers. And there was every reason to believe it.

The differences were mostly in the details. With no wasted motion, Lewis had reshaped the roster, hardened the players' commitments, overhauled the weight room, intensified the practices, pumped up the professionalism and even, as the crowd saw when the team took the field against the Denver Broncos, redesigned the Bengals' uniforms. The pants were black.

And then the game started; and, about half an hour later, the boos. It was all too familiar. It was Denver 30, Cincinnati 10.

The next game was also lost; and the next. Said Brian Simmons, the veteran linebacker, "We knew it wasn't going to be a wave of the wand. We knew it was a process."

It was the fourth time in five seasons that the Bengals had started out 0-3. Among those, however, it would be the first time that they recovered from such a burdensome beginning.

The signature victory—the one in which their wins finally caught up with their losses—came at home against Kansas City. For the third time in four weeks, Cincinnati had taken down a division leader, a heady stretch that so emboldened wide receiver Chad Johnson that he predicted the upset over the undefeated Chiefs. But it was Peter Warrick, the Bengals' other showy receiver, who made the day by returning a punt for a spectacular touchdown. And he, in the spirit of his irrepressible running mate, predicted it.

"Right before I ran it back," claimed the former superstar from Florida State, "I looked at T.J. (Houshmandzadeh) and said, 'I'm about to seal this one with a kiss.' We're a whole new team. It's going down, man. I'm talking about Cincinnati, baby!"

The entire league, in fact, was doing that. And city. The next day, 400 people lined up at the stadium for Chad Johnson's autograph session. Rudi Johnson, meanwhile, with 165 rushing yards against Kansas City after relieving Dillon with 182 the week before against Houston, was developing his own devoted following, consisting in part of rejuvenated Bengals fans who shouted "Roo-Dee!" every time he toted the ball in his straightforward, unassuming style.

Victories followed at San Diego and Pittsburgh, giving Cincinnati four in a row and six in seven Sundays. Beating the Steelers actually put Lewis's reconstituted team in first place for a while—until it lost at Baltimore the following week, leaving the field to the sing-songy chant of, "Same old Bengals . . ."

But they weren't, of course. The next week, Roo-Dee had another 163 yards and Cincinnati beat San Francisco to put itself in position to make the playoffs. It would happen if victories could be secured over St. Louis and the unthreatening Cleveland Browns.

The Bengals, however, were up to neither task. The season-ending loss to the Browns, their detested and retooling rivals, was especially disillusioning. The consolation was that, even at 8-8, the Bengals, for the first time in seven years, had shown themselves not to be losers. It was definitely something.

"It was a good year," said Lewis, and none could disagree. "Not a great year; a good year."

And the next was just like it, win-wise. Depending on one's perspective, the second straight 8-8 was either a petering out or an auspicious prelude. The difference, for those of the latter school, was the quarterback, and the promise personified in him.

THINKING LONG-TERM at the possible expense of immediate prospects, Lewis had named Palmer as his starting quarterback well before the 2004 season began, and never backed off; not even when, for the second year in a row, the Bengals stood 1-4, their progress in apparent peril.

It was just after midseason when the young passing prince began to show his station. Behind him, the Cincinnati offense put up 58 points on Cleveland. The next week, Palmer ravaged the Ravens for 382 passing yards. The next, he was pressing the Patriots, actually having his way with the team that was about to win another Super Bowl, when his game and season ended with a knee strain. But he was fine—better than fine—for 2005. He was, for much of that season, the hottest quarterback in the NFL.

Nevertheless, and with respect to

Palmer's conspicuous talents, the fact is that circumstances must conspire for a season to develop as Cincinnati's did in 2005. The Bengals, for a change, sported a schedule in their favor, and celebrated it early for a 4-0 record; then 7-2; then—who would have thought?—with two games remaining, 11-3. In the way of things working out, there was also the incidence of patience paying off, Lewis looking awfully good for using his first-ever draft pick on a player who wouldn't enter a game for an entire year. There was the maturation of a manly offensive line, led by the sage and steady Willie Anderson. There was the reliability of Rudi and the charm of Chad and all in all an offense, pulled together by Palmer, that disguised the deficiencies of the Cincinnati defense, which at least had its moments.

Validation came, as it had to, against the Pittsburgh Steelers. It came, as few believed it could, in Pittsburgh, with the division title on the line. The December victory represented (1) the ninth of the season, making it the Bengals' first winning one in 16 years; (2) the virtual clinching of the division title; and (3) a brash statement as to where the franchise now and suddenly stood in relation to one of the league's most eminent. The Steelers had been surmounted.

Or so it seemed. When the playoffs finally returned to the land they had forgotten, they brought with them, of all teams, Pittsburgh. With a late flourish, the Steelers had salvaged their season. And Cincinnati was ready, in all respects.

The town was so orange, it could have been peeled and quartered. The team was so confident, Chad Johnson didn't have to say a word. Palmer was so prepared that, on the second play from scrimmage, his first pass of the playoffs, he lofted a long beauty to Chris Henry, good for 66 yards and a roar that rolled along the river and a rousing rush of possibility perceived. This could really happen.

But no, goodness no, that couldn't happen. Surely, Palmer couldn't be injured as badly as it looked as he writhed on the artificial turf. So electric had been the deep completion that few had seen Pittsburgh's Kimo von Oelhoffen, a former Bengal, yank Palmer's knee as the pass set forth from the young hero's hand.

There remains, among Bengals and their faithful, and in spite of the Super Bowl championship that the Steelers went on to win, no doubt as to what the outcome would have been that day had Palmer's knee not been ripped asunder. Kitna did his professional best in the name of the cause, staking Cincinnati to a 17-7 lead that was reduced to 17-14 by halftime; but even then—long before the Steelers scored 24 straight, inevitable points—a muted, palpable pall had settled over Paul Brown Stadium. Seldom has such a store of enthusiasm —a fervor suppressed by more than a decade of disenfranchisement, and gathered up for the coming of that very afternoon—been so suddenly, summarily hushed. Seldom have such evident prospects been so swiftly crushed.

And yet, even so, the season's events left behind an unassailable sense of which direction the Bengals were heading. It was a faith-based feeling, newly and thirstily embraced, that Lewis would not allow even the seriousness of Palmer's injury to bump his team off the byway he had been so diligently building.

He would, however, need guardrails.

—Lonnie Wheeler

the Road Back

The camp

In the NFL, summer camp is when big men take over small colleges. It is also when football players wish they had chosen baseball. For their preseason training, baseball teams repair to warm places in late winter, then knock off early in the afternoon so the fellas don't get too fatigued from all that tossing and stretching. Football teams do it in August, twice a day.

Until 1997, the Bengals chose Wilmington College in tree-draped Ohio for their getting ready. Apparently, Wilmington wasn't hot enough. Now they deposit their extra poundage in the bluegrass of Georgetown College in steamy central Kentucky. It's important, of course, that diversions are kept at a safe distance.

On the whole, Wilmington enjoyed better football in its 29 summers. A couple Super Bowl teams were featured attractions. But, due to the commercial genius of the NFL, training camp has become a more fashionable spectator sport. You can get hotdogs and T-shirts and even autographs, if you know where to lie in wait.

You also get players in better shape than the old-timers were. Generally, this owes to the extra spring mini-camps and such that have been approved in recent years. And with the Bengals, specifically, the relative readiness is a reflection of the off-season regimen that Marvin Lewis has rather strongly suggested.

To that end, there's a slogan emblazoned across the top of the Bengals' glittery weight room at Paul Brown Stadium. It says, "As iron sharpens iron, so one man sharpens another." It's all about working together, and as often as possible.

The same, of course, applies to training camp, which is where Jon Kitna had undisturbed weeks to show Carson Palmer what it takes. Training camp is where Rudi Johnson looked so good long before he got to do the same in a real game. It's where David Pollack, the team's top draft choice in 2005, would have learned to play linebacker if he had signed and shown up in time.

In eschewing Georgetown altogether, Pollack revived an old Bengals tradition concerning training camp. There was nearly always a tedious watch on which rookies would make it there, and when. In 1984, their No. 1 selection, Ricky Hunley—ironically, now one of Lewis's assistants—extended his holdout into the regular season, ultimately forcing Cincinnati to trade him away.

Palmer was the most pleasant and conspicuous exception. Since the Bengals, by virtue of their lousiness in 2002, possessed the league's first draft choice in 2003—which was Lewis's first year as head coach—they had the luxury of negotiating with and signing their man before the draft actually took place. Even so, it was startling to see them come to terms so summarily with a Heisman Trophy winner.

"I'm nowhere near my potential. And I'm very, very good right now. I always have something to prove. What I did last year is nothing. I erase my memory. I'm a rookie all over again..."
—The Chadmeister

"The point here is suffering. SUFFERING
IS THE OBJECT. You get reacquainted with it
in July, so by November, it's second nature."
—Paul Daugherty, *Enquirer* columnist

But it was a fine thing for all concerned, and it meant that Palmer could go mini-camping in the spring and show up at Georgetown with an actual clue as to what he was doing. Scott County's top tourist attraction that summer was Palmer throwing long balls and sideline patterns.

Beyond the likes of that, there's always the possibility of a good training-camp fight between a big veteran defensive lineman and a big rookie offensive lineman, or vice versa. Football players tend to get a little edgy when people are trying to take their jobs away and it's really hot and they're getting smacked in places that don't have pads.

For the more astute observers of training camp, there are also plenty of mind games to pass the time with, such as determining which of the speedy free-agent rookie receivers is going to look great all summer and generate lots of excitement and finally win a spot on the practice squad; or trying to identify which Brown family member is under which straw hat.

Camp is the time for the perfection of arcane exercises you might never see anywhere short of the Discovery Channel and turf contests between heated elk. Here, the world narrows to blocker and tackler, and the high-rent district is wherever someone is still upright. David Pollack, recently of the University of Georgia, is seen here having his credentials tested.

Student Pollack...

Clothesline 101...

Class dismissed.

Homework

Freddie Milons, the great multi-use wide receiver

from Alabama, survived the Bengals' practice

squad in 2004, survived the summer camp

of 2005, then was a victim of numbers

before the exhibition season ended,

proving that there *are* worse things

than camp. But not *many*.

"When Carson was coming out of college," Jon Kitna told *Sports Illustrated*, "you'd hear people say, 'He's not the brightest guy. It's going to take him three to four years before he understands an NFL system.' But Carson was getting it about halfway through '04..."

Barkl

fresh meat
The rookies

At the University of Georgia, David Pollack was such an overwhelming defensive lineman that the coaches would sometimes hold him out of practice so the offense could actually run through its plays. Socially skilled and famously dedicated to his craft, Pollack was the first two-time winner of the Ted Hendricks Award, given to the best defensive end in the college ranks, as well as the recipient of the Lombardi Award, which said that he was the nation's best lineman. He was also the Bengals' first-round draft choice in 2005.

The second was his Georgia teammate, Odell Thurman, an aggressive but imperfect middle linebacker whose flaws once got him kicked off the squad for a while. Thurman was not nearly as polished as Pollack, but he made a good choice when it came to signing his rookie contract. He did it quickly, becoming an immediate starter and wasting no time in joining the illustrious circle of Cincinnati's second-round successes, a company that includes Boomer Esiason, Chad Johnson, Corey Dillon, Cris Collinsworth, Ickey Woods, Carl Pickens, Dan Ross, Pete Johnson, Bill Bergey and Tommy Casanova. (It was Pollack, though, who was called on Draft Day, "a Boomer Esiason personality for the defense.")

Then Pollack opted to do what so many of the Bengals' first-round choices have done over the years. He kept himself out of training camp while the deal was being bickered. He missed it all. That was a particularly unfortunate idea in light of the fact that he was drafted not

as a defensive end but as a linebacker, which meant that he had to acclimate himself to a new universe and a new position at the same time. Unlike Thurman (and also second-year defensive end Robert Geathers, another former teammate at Georgia), he was not a starter when the season began.

Pollack did manage to make six tackles in the opener at Cleveland, the same team-leading total as Thurman. But the latter—wearing the number 51 formerly sported by Takeo Spikes—came up with an interception, as well, and, to his delight, had the media massed around his locker when the game was over and the victory secured.

"It's going to be a new day for number 51," boasted Thurman, which is something he was wont, smiling, to do. "Who's Takeo?"

As the season progressed, the low-riding linebacker showed a snappy penchant for picking off both the ball-carrier and the ball, whether it was lugged or thrown.

"He gets to the ball," noted Brian Simmons,

Rookie wide receiver Tab Perry
earned himself a place on special
teams, returning all but two
kickoffs during the season.
His 1,562 return yards
(a 24.4 average) broke a
13-year single-season record
(held by Tremain Mack). His
94-yard kickoff return during
the third quarter of the December
4 Pittsburgh game gave for the
Steelers a kick in the head
Rudi went to score,
putting the Bengals
ahead for good.
Or at least until
that fateful
Wildcard Playoff
game on January 8.

the steady veteran on Thurman's flank, "and he brings his hat with him."

By midseason, he was favored to be the NFL Defensive Rookie of the Year, as well as receiving comparisons (even if premature) to none other than Baltimore's preeminent linebacker Ray Lewis, Thurman's boyhood idol.

Meanwhile, the more ballyhooed Bulldog found some relief from his linebacker-learning when he occasionally lined up at defensive end to rush the passer, doing so in such a way as to portend headier things in store for him. As it was, Pollack's rookie production was ahead of the curve for the first-rounders of the Marvin Lewis era, Carson Palmer having been apprenticed in his initial season and Chris Perry having been hurt. The others, though, had better excuses.

And so it went with these Georgia bookends. Pollack was the trophy case linebacker, the consensus All-American. But Thurman had the better year. All in all, it portended greater things for both, and— more important—the Cincinnati defense.

Against Green Bay, the Bengals intercepted Bret Favre five times, which had never before happened, at least in a regular season game. And Odell Thurman had two of them. That made four, and it was still October. All four came off tipped balls. "I CALL HIM 'TIP DRILL,'" said Deltha O'Neal. He was only the second Bengal to win NFL Rookie of the Month honors (Corey Dillon was the other), and the first defensive Bengal to win since the award began in 1996. Soon, they were calling him "the defensive version of Chad Johnson."

In 2004, when Chris Henry was at West Virginia, he was called "the best pure deep threat in college football." He had most everything: size, speed, and strength. The problem was that he did not confine his sense of spectacle to the gridiron. When the question was, "Would you rather play on grass or Astroturf?" Henry seemed to have the wrong answer. Whoops. But just look at him (at right) against the Vikings in that 37-8 Bengal win.

Dance with me

You put yo right foot in, you put yo right foot out

and you shake it all about...

The Man

It's not true, as many Bengals fans have come to believe, that Marvin Lewis is God. But both can be found in the details. Some coaches are charged with rebuilding a roster. Lewis had to construct a whole new culture in Cincinnati, where losing had become systemic, endemic, and seemingly inevitable. His task was one of redefinition.

That included language, nomenclature, and whatever else was associated with the Bengals' wretched recent past, which he was insistent upon disavowing. The 2-14 Bengals were somebody else's. References to previous years or patterns or proclivities had no place in his new order, and were met as sabotaging impositions of a mentality that he had grabbed by the collar and tossed through the saloon doors, with strong advice to stay out.

Whatever was changeable, he changed, whether it was players or practice schedules or the dinner menu. He was everywhere, talking to everybody, doing everything. In many and unexpected ways, Mike Brown had given Lewis the run of the football team; and while that fundamental change was thrilling to many Bengals observers, others wondered how long any man could hold up to all of it.

Lewis, however, took on more. From the moment the Pittsburgh native arrived in 2003 as a dazzling defensive coordinator, he made it his responsibility not only to assemble the personnel he would work with—a job generally under the purview of a general manager, which the Bengals were officially without—but also to rally the surrounding community in the interest of creating a proper NFL atmosphere. For him, there was no task too big (serving as organization spokesman) or small (replacing the stools in the locker room).

So manifest was his attention to detail that faith followed along implicitly, even when Lewis's first team started out 0-3. There was just something different about it. Losing, it somehow seemed, was no longer quite so congruous with the club in the Bengals' locker room. It truly thought better of itself.

The sobering but not surprising reality was that the Bengals' rudely regarded past, having grown so enormously burdensome, would not be easily pitched from the premises. Before long, though, Lewis's details had reached such a critical mass that they began to tip the balance on the scoreboard. In some cities, 8-8 would be an eminently forgettable season. In Cincinnati, it was practically a miracle.

In a mere year, Lewis had succeeded in changing the image of the most maligned franchise in professional sports. Just like that, the Bengals had converted not only the commentators and comedians and radio heads,

"What separates you and gets you over the hump in the NFL is how you finish things. You want to start fast, but you've got to finish."
—Marvin Lewis

but also—and most important—appropriate players of the NFL. In Lewis's first year, a few free agents had entertained the notion of Cincinnati for simply his sake; now, with the Biblical losing very apparently behind it, the team at large was actually somewhat enticing.

It was all a salutary cycle. By redefining the Bengals' culture, Lewis had created a team with the will and wherewithal to make over its image. The spoils of image, in turn, swiftly advanced the reformation of the culture.

Remarkably, none of this was a bit undone when Lewis's second team flattened out at another 8-8; only this time with Carson Palmer at quarterback. Palmer, it was clear, would soon be a superstar. And sooner than imagined.

It came to pass in 2005, and so, by no happenstance, did the Bengals in the playoffs. Palmer's part in it was front and center to an extent that, from undiscerning critics, to him will go the credit for transforming the long-terrible team. But that's not how it went.

Palmer, in truth, was merely foremost among the details that ultimately did it—and they were Marvin Lewis's details.

Lewis brought his own kind of heat to the place that for years had been known as the NFL's Siberia. And then there seemed to be an immediate if unlikely bond between this African-American offspring of a Pennsylvania millworker and the white scion who had inherited his famous father's team but not yet his winning tradition. If by 2005 theirs was not quite a marriage made in heaven, it *did* get them into the playoffs. Heaven, said the long-suffering fans, could wait. At least for another season.

Palmer
The Franchise

The Bengals had drafted David Klingler as a first-round quarterback, and that wasn't so good. They had done the same with Akili Smith, and, oh my, that was worse. And yet, when they signed Carson Palmer even before the 2003 draft—having the first pick overall—they did so amidst cheerful indications that the third time would be the arm.

It wasn't just Palmer's Heisman Trophy that hinted at this. It wasn't his tall Southern California carriage. It wasn't even his willingness to sign-on so speedily. It was, rather, something he said the day he did. "L.A.," confided the nation's top prospect, "is a little too up-tempo for me. I'm a low-key guy. I like being with my family, watching TV, and hanging out. I don't really do a whole lot. I think I'll fit in well here."

He was already married to a Southern Cal soccer goalie. He was already golden in the areas of looks, contract, and reputation. He was, in short, just about everything that the average Bengal decidedly wasn't, a circumstance that only added significance to his refreshing embrace of Cincinnati.

Palmer also wrapped his arms around the program on which Marvin Lewis put him. In his rookie season, he would observe Jon Kitna quarterbacking the Bengals to their first non-losing record in seven years. In his second, Palmer, supplanting Kitna as the Cincinnati starter and abetted by the selfless counsel that Kitna would afford him unfailingly, would demonstrate the stuff required to become one of the best quarterbacks in the NFL. And in his third year (after spending the summer back in California, critiquing movies

which he sometimes starred in and just as often spoiled), he was very much that.

The Bengals, in turn, were very much playoff contenders in 2005, and Lewis wasn't shy about saying why. "Carson is our offense," the coach remarked frankly. "He's so, so talented. No matter what he touches, it turns to gold."

Before the season was over, the Bengals, in that spirit, had heaped more precious metal onto the gifted passer's platter. They extended his contract through 2014, the sum of it being around $118 million. And the deal looked like a bargain when Cincinnati won the AFC North, earning the right to host its first playoff game in 15 years.

Palmer well understood that, for all the numbers and high praise that had come his way during the heady season, he would ultimately be defined by his performance in the playoffs. "All you hear is, 'Tom Brady is 9-0 as a postseason quarterback,' " he said, referring to the Patriots' Super Bowl swashbuckler. "And you hear about (Dan) Marino, and that Peyton (Manning) hasn't gotten to the big one.

"When people talk about quarterbacks of the past, they talk about what happened in the playoffs. That's part of your legacy, and my legacy starts this week."

It started against the Pittsburgh Steelers, with a long, impeccable pass down the right sideline to Chris Henry, good for 66 yards and a swell of confidence in the Bengal fans. And then silence. Palmer was down, with the Steelers' Kimo von Oelhoffen standing awkwardly over him. In a desperate, devastating grab that will remain forever controversial, von Oelhoffen had ended Palmer's season at the knee. Cincinnati's would soon crumple, as well.

Palmer's legacy, as a result, would derive from how he dealt with what happened in the playoffs. And the prospects were not unlike those that attended his arrival three years before. "Carson has the attitude of a superstar, the attitude of a winner," said offensive lineman Willie Anderson, whose wisdom may be measured by the pound. "He has the attitude that I'm sure Michael Jordan had when he broke his foot. That's the kind of attitude of guys who win the Heisman Trophy.

"For him to go have the season he had in his third season, he has to have the kind of attitude that regular guys don't have. Only the elite guys have that kind of temperament. And it's what Carson has."

Around that temperament and that arm and that knee, the Bengals' future would revolve in the best of faith.

In 2005, Carson Palmer threw 32 touchdown passes (against 12 interceptions), on his way to completing 345 of 509 passes (67.8 percent) for 3,836 yards. Only Peyton Manning was ahead of Palmer's 101.1 passing rating, and Palmer was fifth in the league MVP voting. Said Paul Daugherty, "His head is so level, you could shoot pool on it."

Sports Illustrated's 2004 pro football issue asked: "Can Carson Palmer cut it in Cincinnati?" Said Palmer, as though he needed a defense (other than his own, on the field), "It's natural to want to look like the Number One pick, but that's why a lot of young guys struggle. We have so many talented players that we don't need a superstar at quarterback. We just need somebody who can do his job." With that said, he did both—he did his job *and* he looked like a superstar.

When the Bengals scouted Palmer, his accuracy
was already legend, said *ESPN* magazine: "When told
to hit a receiver on a 35-yard fly route, Palmer would
ask, with a straight face, 'You want that
on the upfield nipple or downfield nipple?'"
He had other accuracies, too. When Willie Anderson
asked him about winning the Heisman at USC,
Palmer shrugged off the question.
"Ray Lewis doesn't care about the Heisman," he said.

STEWART

86

WILLIAMS

63

"What's Fo

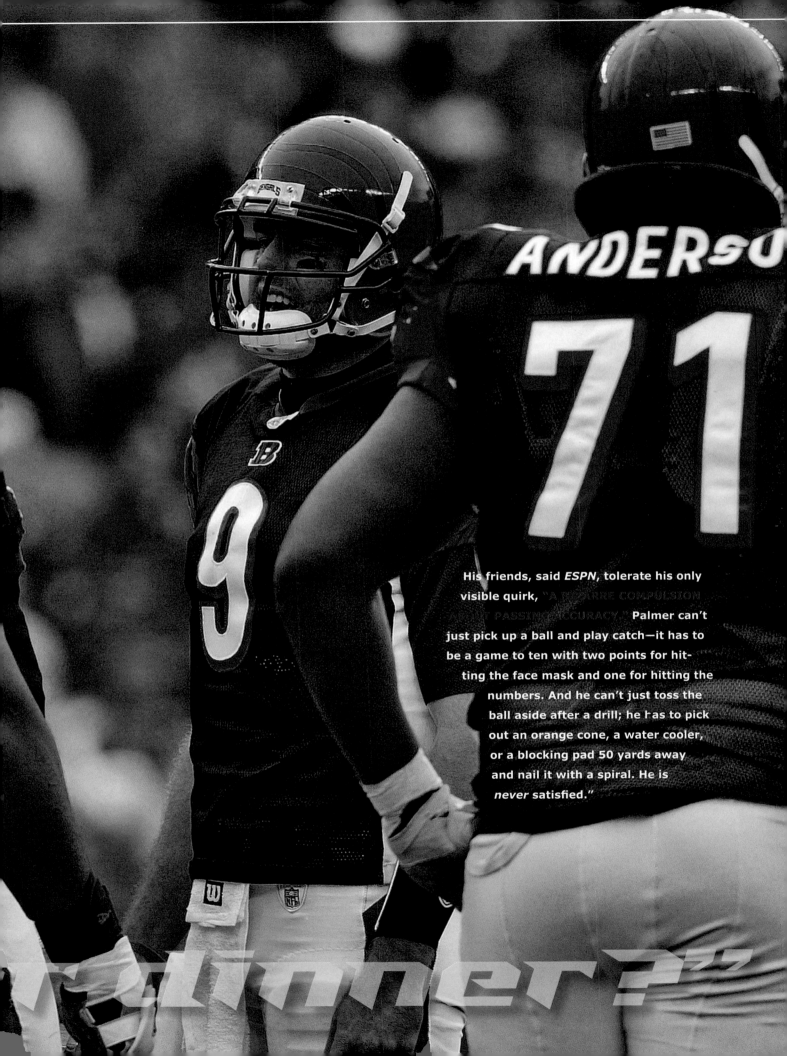

His friends, said *ESPN*, tolerate his only visible quirk, "A BIZARRE COMPULSION ABOUT PASSING ACCURACY." Palmer can't just pick up a ball and play catch—it has to be a game to ten with two points for hitting the face mask and one for hitting the numbers. And he can't just toss the ball aside after a drill; he has to pick out an orange cone, a water cooler, or a blocking pad 50 yards away and nail it with a spiral. He is *never* satisfied."

Kitna The mainstay

Jon Kitna had everything it takes to be an unsung hero. It was he who tided the Bengals over until Carson Palmer was ready for professional quarterbacking. It was he who graciously stepped aside when the time came, who best-friended the Heisman Trophy winner and tutored and counseled and championed him. And all of that was supremely fortuitous for the Bengals and the stuff, really, of unsung heroism, except for one thing. Kitna was *sung*.

His praises were hummed from paper to paper, show to show, mouth to mouth. His hands were too small, his feet too nervous, his arm too ordinary to take the Bengals where they were evidently heading—everyone knew that—but in their sudden ascent back to NFL normalcy, Kitna was a noble enabler; and vastly appreciated as that.

He could have made it difficult. And he knew all about difficult. He well knew how divided quarterbacks divided teams. He knew that the Bengals had never gotten over the three-ring debacle of 2002, when he, Akili Smith, and Gus Frerotte had reported to training camp on even, awkward footing. And in spite of the quality of his work in 2003, when Kitna was a Pro Bowl alternate and NFL Comeback Player of the Year, he knew that he mustn't fuss when Palmer's day arrived. "I hate that about people in this league," he said. "When they want to gripe and moan all the time when they don't agree with their situation."

Such an attitude, of course, should not be exceptional. But it was, and he was. He would say that it was his Christianity that made him so, because he almost unfailingly made a point of introducing it into his public conversations; and while a lot of people wouldn't really respond to that part, they responded to Kitna.

They responded to him so faithfully, in fact, that he became no common backup quarterback; not in role and certainly not in perception. Even when Kitna didn't play a down in 2004, few doubted that he was among the most valuable Bengals. And the same went for 2005.

What a story it would have been if he had led his team to that December victory against the Steelers. He had it going for a while there. When Palmer went down and couldn't get up after his sensational first pass of the playoffs, Kitna came on like a fairy tale. He had Cincinnati in the lead at halftime.

In the end, it was a reminder of why Palmer was Palmer and Kitna wasn't. The Steelers huddled well at halftime, persuading themselves that it was only Kitna's arm on Kitna's body that they were dealing with—that Kitna, come to think of it, had taken Cincinnati as far as he was able to. His work here was effectively done; and so, with that, were the Bengals.

A few months later, Kitna was gone, lured to Detroit by the possibility of a starter's job and the chance to make another team—and another city—better.

After Kitna's finest season—3,591 passing yards, 26 TDs—he was replaced by the emerging Palmer. Betraying only a trace of the disappointment he surely felt, he said to Marvin Lewis, "I made that decision tough on you, didn't I?" Then as mentor and friend to Palmer, Kitna—the most talented carrier of clipboards in the league—proceeded to show NFL players, coaches, and fans how to handle yourself with grace and dignity when the $10 million whiz kid comes to take your place.

Jon Kitna was an undrafted free agent by Seattle in 1996, went to NFL Europe and led Barcelona to the 1998 World Bowl Championship, then started for Seattle in 1999 when the Seahawks went 9-7 and won the AFC Western Division Championship. In 2003 he was the NFL's Comeback Player of the Year. The moral? It's hard to keep a good man down.

Two-Eight

As the leading runner in Bengals history, Corey Dillon should have left behind nostalgic snapshots. Instead, there remains the image of, say, September, 2002, when Cincinnati was driving toward the Cleveland goal and Dillon excused himself, walking somewhat gingerly back to the locker room.

Dick LeBeau, the unfortunate coach at the time, later referred to the untimely malady as a "uniform constriction." As he explained it, "Corey couldn't get comfortable in his uniform."

And there you have him. Great as he was in it, Dillon could never get comfortable in a Cincinnati Bengals uniform.

It started even before it actually started, when Dillon went undrafted in 1997's first round and fell to the Bengals in the second. He was so angry, so offended, that he wouldn't take their call.

Angry was just his way. Back in Seattle, he was arrested nine times between the ages of 13 and 17, including at least a time or two for just being with the wrong people in the same kind of place. He was angry with the police for not believing him. He was angry at reporters for unsealing his juvenile record. He was angry at the University of Washington for badmouthing him before the draft. He was angry at the NFL for letting him slide all the way to the Bengals. And after a couple years in Cincinnati —after he had broken Jim Brown's rookie rushing record for a single game—he was angry, of course, at the Bengals, declaring that he would rather flip burgers than continue in a Cincinnati uniform.

Two years after that—a year after he had broken Walter Payton's all-time record for yards in a single game—the Bengals' best player smiled and signed back up.

"It was just," Dillon said, "that I had a greater purpose in Cincinnati than anywhere else. It kind of made it easier for me to stay with the Bengals and try to turn the program around."

He *was* the program, more or less. Running behind such stalwarts as Willie Anderson and Rich Braham, the big back lowered his head, ran angry, and broke all the franchise records. And then Marvin Lewis arrived and the team became legitimate and it should have been a wonderful time for Dillon. He should have played the role of the long-suffering star, the loyal, enduring hero to whom the spoils of victory were way overdue. He shouldn't have been angry anymore.

But when the Bengals became Lewis's team, they were no longer Dillon's. That was evident when he skipped the first mini-camp, then, with Lewis looking on soberly, apologized at the next one. He missed a game because of a groin injury, and another because of a traffic accident on the way to the stadium. Rudi Johnson took his place. The crowd cheered Rudi's name. The press gushed about how refreshingly different Rudi was than the Pro Bowler he was replacing. One strange day,

Dillon, apparently weary of saying the right things, wandered into the media room and poured out a startling soliloquy of personal woe, asking, in the process, to be traded. The team, meanwhile, was playing its best football in more than a decade.

Later, even as the Bengals were straining to reach the playoffs, he made it clear that his seventh season in Cincinnati would be his last. "I wasn't part of the growth this year, in many people's eyes," he said. "They kind of made their bed and chose who they wanted to roll with. I came back, played my tail off, did whatever I could do to help the team win. Now it's time to make some business decisions. Me being the CEO of Dillon Incorporated, I'm going to take care of my business. It's time for me to move on. It's time."

When the final game was over—a deflating defeat to the Cleveland Browns—Dillon flung his shoulder pads into the crowd. Not long after that, he went on national television wearing an Oakland Raiders uniform—mind you, he was still officially a Bengal—and said terrible things about Willie Anderson, of all people. The Bengals sent him to New England for, ironically, a second-round draft choice.

Dillon had managed, somehow, to put in seven big-time seasons without changing a bit.

For most of his seven years here—and it could be argued that they were as good as any seven years that any player has contributed to the Cincinnati franchise—THE BENGALS WERE DROP-DEAD AWFUL. Dillon's roughshod running, in light of that, earned him plenty of admiration, not to mention records. He was a ferocious and remarkably productive perseverer.

Bad Corey has already become a collectible, Paul Daugherty tells us. "A bigtime player in the Cincinnati memorabilia market owns his driver's license, acquired when Dillon threw it at a clerk at a drive-through beverage mart, snarling: 'DON'T YOU KNOW WHO I AM?'" *Now* he does.

If it was a test—two dissenters looking for greener turf—then Lewis passed it.

Dillon headed for New England, and linebacker Takeo Spikes (left), the team's

consistent leading tackler, shuffled off to Buffalo. In the process, Lewis appeared

mightily unruffled at losing his kingpin on each side of the ball. Maybe it was

because he had just become the first person in the history of the franchise—other

than The Family—to make a personnel decision. Maybe it was because he, Marvin

Lewis, actually *wanted* to be in Cincinnati.

So Takeo *did* become All-Pro in Buffalo.

He was *still* in Buffalo.

7-eleven

Chad Johnson, as he was known and loved, became illegal before the 2006 football season. The NFL masterminds, self-appointed social watchdogs for our autumn Sundays, got together and, in what is referred to by some as the Chad rule, determined that, after touchdowns, there will be no more marriage proposals, Riverdances, or putting with pylons. Celebrations will henceforth be more traditional. Duller, in other words.

But if the league is to take away Johnson . . . well, the Bengals receiver is accustomed to dealing with that every week. Opposing defenses had already targeted him as their top priority when playing Cincinnati, the object of their attention and double-teams. They had decided, in effect, that number 85 is as good as he claims to be.

In 2005, to quantify himself as "unblanketable" and validate his self-assessed nickname of 7-Eleven (because he's always open), Johnson taped to his locker a list of the cornerbacks who would be assigned to cover him throughout the season, with room provided for checkmarks indicating whether or not they were able to. It was a classic Chad gag, a disarming blend of humor and puffery, and of course, in the end, it verified what he so often proclaimed. "I'm an unstoppable force," he said, setting a sober standard for himself. "It's mission impossible. You can do nothing to stop me. Seriously."

The numbers—the occasions, for instance, in which he has led the conference in receptions and yardage—support him only to an extent. There have been times, it must be said, when good teams have succeeded in minimizing his catches, his breakaways, his touchdowns, his electric effect. In committing their resources to doing so, however, they have discreetly acknowledged the narrowness of the gap between Johnson's mouth and his talent.

Football, for him, has become self-expression in a fundamental way. He came out of the troubled Liberty City neighborhood of Miami, with little interest in other honest pursuits. "If it weren't for football," he once said, "I'd be one of three places. I'd be dead, I'd be in jail, or —what's the other thing?—I'd be selling drugs. I cannot sit here and picture myself, 25 years old —someone who did not like school, who was not successful at school, who was no academic genius —without football. What would I be able to do? Football had to do it. Football is my savior."

If, then, Johnson's braggadocio is not always genuine, his joy assuredly is. His dedication is. And the merger of the two is what makes him indisputably special.

Clearly, he is more than can be observed clearly. Fans see his gold teeth (when he chooses to wear them); they see the bottles of Pepto-

Bismol he sent to the Cleveland cornerbacks (because covering him would surely make them sick to their stomachs); they see him guaranteeing a victory over undefeated Kansas City, which came to pass; they see him giving CPR to the football in the end zone; and they see him holding up signs asking the league not to fine him for holding up signs; but they don't see him in Marvin Lewis's doorway in the middle of May. They don't see him taking extra repetitions in practice. They don't see him sleeping at Paul Brown Stadium.

"I'm not a distraction," he said, to that effect. "I'm a ballplayer." Of course, he also said, once, that he's not a ballplayer, he's an entertainer. Johnson never claimed to be consistent. He never claimed to be any particular thing, and that alone.

"There are three parts to me," he declared, actually naming only two. "There's Chad, the football player. There's Chad, the serious player on Sunday. (Okay, that's one.) And there's Chad, who keeps the fans excited, which they've never been around here."

But he's very right; there are at least three parts to him. The third could be the Chad who, uncontrollably frustrated, reportedly had a tiff with a coach during halftime of the playoff game against the Steelers. It could be the Chad who grew up with his grandmother and still doesn't know how or why his grandfather was killed in 1994. It could be the Chad who grew up idolizing his football-starring cousins, Samari Rolle and Keyshawn Johnson. It could be the Chad with tears in his eyes after a bad game. It could be the Chad who accepted the new celebration legislation philosophically, determined to find a way around it and still have some characteristic fun.

It could be any number of Chads that the NFL can't stop with its silly rules.

So how much celebration *is* there in the celebrant,

this brash yet still sweet-natured man of the moment

who spends most of the off-season with his grandmother?

Says his biographer, Paul Daugherty, "There are jocks

who don't talk and jocks who have nothing to say.

There are those from whom you extract syllables like

like platinum from the earth. AND THERE IS JOHNSON.

Open the notebook and give the man some room."

So the question: Is there *anything* that will

make the speechifier speechless? *Maybe*.

Before the afternoon of September 18, 2005—definitely not a Viking afternoon—was over, the boys from Minnesota might as well have been, say, the Bikes. Back-pedaling, see? On the second play, Palmer found Chad on a 70-yard deep post: TOUCHDOWN. Now, when he said, as he did, "I'm not coverable," the fans were believing him. And so were the DBs. So it was 2-0 in Cincinnati, soon to be 4-0. "Two-and-oh means nothing," Chad said. Well, not everything, Chad, but *something*.

"'I GOT

Something might be gaining on Chad.

Then again, probably not.

you,

In Johnson's last three seasons—all Pro Bowl years—he has caught 282 passes for 4,061 yards and 28 touchdowns. He is, as sportswriter Mark Curnutte pointed out, "entertaining without demeaning opponents or the game. He has danced to within an inch of the going-too-far line but has not stepped across it, all the while evolving into an ESPN highlight staple...he has helped bring the fun back to the No Fun League, and he has done so in the most unlikely of places—buttoned-down Cincinnati."

Before the Indianapolis game in November of 2005, Chad said, "I'm about to get myself in trouble. I guarantee—I'm serious—I guarantee that I will not be stopped." Then he went out and caught eight passes for 189 yards. Truth in advertising. Wrote his biographer, Paul Daugherty, in *Chad: i Can't be Stopped*, "He has been told forever by coaches that his talking makes things harder for everyone, including him. The day Johnson believes that is the day he trades his shoulder pads for a shuffleboard cue." Said Chad himself: "I talk, you get mad, play as good as you can and I *still* beat you. Do you know what that does for my game?"

"The glow from the noonday sun bounces off his eight or ten gold teeth and lands like a spotlight across his wide-open face. Didn't he stop wearing the gold caps after one of Marvin Lewis' fatherly lectures? Turns out, he didn't. 'I mean business' when the caps are on, Chad explained. 'The gold only goes in on the field. It's like Superman. He doesn't walk around in the suit. When it's time for business, he's in the red and blue. The gold defines me. I'm always shining. I continue to keep this organization shining.'"

—Paul Daugherty

You wouldn't know it from the festive crowd, but this was the day the cheering stopped—January 8, 2006, Pittsburgh 31, Cincinnati 17. But having been denied so long— and this time so cruelly—everyone knew one thing. They *would* be back.

The wheels

In 2004, which, by the riddance of Corey Dillon, was Rudi Johnson's first year as the Bengals' full-time running back, Johnson had an opportunity, in the final game, to break Dillon's single-season team rushing record. Willie Anderson, the distinguished right tackle behind whom Rudi did much of his best work, was quite aware of the occasion. He was quite aware, also, of the pain in his knee, which would require surgery as soon as the season was over. Inasmuch as the Bengals maintained no playoff possibilities, it would have been perfectly acceptable for Anderson to take the day off in deference to better health. In Johnson's behalf, he refused to do so until the record had changed hands.

It wasn't because both players had come to Cincinnati from Auburn University. It wasn't because Dillon was the man being supplanted. Nor was it because the record would be of particular benefit to Anderson himself; he, in fact, had been a lead blocker for Dillon, too.

It was just Rudi. It was just the respect that Johnson commanded from teammates and football fans and anyone who appreciates a professional athlete who doesn't act like one, except on the field; who doesn't strut, who doesn't style, who doesn't complain, who doesn't seek personal gain.

"He's just a worker and a plugger," said Big Willie. "We all call him Grimy. He's just a grimy guy. I can't tell you the things he does, because the man's had some success and he could be working on his image right now. But he's earned the nickname."

In 2005, Johnson broke his team record again, by four yards, and did it with fewer carries. His small-chunk, straight-ahead production was what the Bengals needed for an air-based, big-play offense that connected Chad Johnson to Carson Palmer. To that end, it was categorically telling when, on the morning of the day that the trade of Dillon would be announced, Lewis was asked in what way his team had improved, and he replied, with unusual directness, "Number one, we're better at running back."

With heavy-duty Rudi taking the handoffs, the Bengals, sure enough, were better on Sundays, on the field; and with Dillon in Massachusetts, they were better on Wednesdays and Thursdays, in the locker room. Unlike his prolific predecessor, Johnson was a player who, by his efficacious selflessness, slipped naturally

into the good graces of his coaches, his blockers, and his public. "Roo-Dee!" chanted the latter. "First down!" answered the ref.

It was all so unforeseen, really. In his one season (his junior year) at Auburn, Johnson had been Southeastern Conference Player of the Year; but the Bengals, nevertheless, found him still available in the fourth round of the draft, too short and slow to have gone any higher. They felt no urgency for a running back, what with Dillon doing so well, and for two years Johnson was mostly a preseason and special-teams player. Only when Dillon turned up periodically hurt in 2003 did his stocky understudy receive a real chance to run the ball. He promptly became the first Bengal ever to rush for 150 yards three times in the same season, in all gaining nearly a thousand.

"I'm a smashmouth guy," is how Johnson explained it. "Me and the offensive line, that's what we're accustomed to doing."

And for him, the line is only too happy to.

Roo-dee

He's a taller man...

...for this 2003 stretch against Seattle.

Roo-dee

"Sure. I'd like every guy to be like Rudi Johnson, who honors himself by dropping the ball to the turf when he scores. *I've done this before. I WILL DO IT AGAIN.* That is the height of cool."

—Paul Daugherty, on Rudi Johnson

"Rudi, the hardest-working man in show business...
the man is 220 POUNDS OF PURPOSE. When he's not working,
he's working. If anybody else starts riding that stationary bike
behind the Bengals bench, I get ticked off. That's *Rudi's* bike."
—Paul Daugherty

It was a special teams kind of moment—Gregory Gall came from behind the Packers' bench, cleared the 9-foot wall, bounced off a cart, then took flight straight for Brett Favre, who thought he had seen about all there is to see in the NFL. Never, though, had the champion of cheeseheads had a fan snatch the ball from his hands as he stood in the pocket.

The previous week had been awful. The Bengals had traveled to Baltimore to determine which team would take control of the AFC North as the 2003 season rolled into its final month, and it wasn't even close. As the beaten Cincinnatians straggled off the field, Ravens fans serenaded them with, "Same old Bengals . . ."

To make it worse, Levi Jones, Cincinnati's outstanding young left tackle, had torn cartilage in his right knee. The next day, he had arthroscopic surgery. Tuesday, he showed up at Paul Brown Stadium on crutches. Sunday morning, as winter blew through and the San Francisco 49ers were gearing up in the other locker room, Jones was pulling on his pads and inspiring his teammates with unsuppressed enthusiasm.

"It's cold, it's snowing, the ground is messed up, his knee is bad," said Willie Anderson, the other tackle. "You really don't feel like jumping around. Then you see him over there, emotional like he always is, and you got to be in the game."

This, however, was not an easy game to stay in. Not the way the points were piling up in drifts.

The Bengals' first touchdown was produced by Chad Johnson, whose previous scores had led to various celebrations that had led to $55,000 in disciplinary charges from the NFL. This time, Johnson was ready. Setting the ball down innocently, he ran to the stadium's back wall, where he had stashed on orange sign that he now held aloft. It said, "Dear NFL, Please don't fine me again! Merry Christmas."

The Bengals led 21-17 at halftime, but only because the 49ers were handling the ball as if they were wearing mittens. They fumbled twice in the first two quarters, their holiday generosity encouraging Cincinnati to try to grind out the game with Rudi Johnson's running, which looked like an even better idea with every play that Jones survived.

Roo-Dee had been a bit player until Corey Dillon began to come and go for various reasons. Three times already that season, Johnson had rushed for more than 100 yards in a game. Twice, he had gained more than 150. This time, he did that in the second half, when he dodged snowflakes for 163 yards and two touchdowns, which still weren't enough to salt the game away. It was necessary that he also recover an onside kick with just over a minute to play. That finally did it, 41-38.

It was the most points the Bengals had ever allowed while winning, a peculiarity that was superseded the next season when they beat the Cleveland Browns 58-48 in an even more preposterous game.

Of deeper importance was that the San Francisco victory was the eighth of Marvin Lewis's first year as head coach, keeping alive Cincinnati's playoff hopes, ensuring a .500 record for the first time since 1996, and debunking the hurtful lyrics that had offended the players' ears in Baltimore.

While the weather outside seemed frightful, it held no fear for Shayne Graham. He was two field goals-for-two, and five extra points-for-five.

Tory James (26), defensive end Duane Clemons (92), and linebacker Brian Simmons (56) hung together for a tough win over the 49ers. Simmons led the Bengals in 2003 with 78 solo tackles, and seven of them came in the 49er game. His two fumble recoveries stopped two San Francisco deep threats. The Bengals overcame a 502-yard offensive effort by the 49ers, thereby becoming the first 2003 NFL team to win after allowing 500 yards. The Bengals also won their fifth straight at home. "LOSING HURTS NOW," said Marvin Lewis, "and we don't like the taste of it."

Here's Corey Dillon in training for New England winters-to-come. Although in this game, Rudi got the yards—174 of them—and Dillon got the flu. Usually, when facing Dillon, *others* found themselves on the receiving end of illness. Dillon didn't get arm-tackled. Tackling Dillon that way, in fact, was the best way to *lose* an arm. Said the running back himself, "I'M 70 PERCENT SECOND EFFORT. Since Pop Warner, coaches instilled in me, 'Keep your legs moving, your eyes open, your head up.'" Sportswriter Paul Daugherty said that Dillon ran *mean*. "It's amazing he did so well here," he said, "considering he had to carry the football *and* the boulder on his shoulder."

Rudi came on in relief and, in the second half alone, ran for 163 yards. "HIT IT AND GIT IT," said Rudi, after a 49-yard score on fourth-and-one, behind an Eric Steinbach block.

Hut hut

The center, Rich Braham, had surgery on his elbow during a bye week, timing it so that he didn't miss a game. One season, he suffered from a herniated disc in his neck, but didn't miss any games for that, either. The year before that, he had two knee surgeries and started the last seven games. He once played a dozen games on a broken toe. A joint was taken out of his little finger, but he didn't even think about missing any games for that.

The left tackle, Levi Jones, had to leave a game with a torn meniscus in his right knee, and in his absence the substitute tackle was called twice for false starts and was beaten twice for sacks, one of which led to a fumble. Taking note of that, Jones made sure he was in the lineup the next week, and stayed in it the whole game. It was six days after arthroscopic surgery.

The left guard, Eric Steinbach, played an entire season on an elbow that he couldn't straighten, a rather significant impediment when attempting to block 320-pound defensive linemen.

The right tackle, Willie Anderson, played a full season—his fifth in a row without missing a game—with what he called "the hole in my bone" and the Bengals described as torn knee cartilage. He had it repaired, skipped the Pro Bowl, spent the next few months in a pilates studio with a bunch of somewhat smaller women, then played all the next season.

Anderson thinks Jones should be chosen for the Pro Bowl, too; and before long, he probably will be. Steinbach plays at about

the same level. Bobbie Williams, the right guard, is the strongest Bengal, one of the most dependable, and the one most likely to make your hand disappear when he shakes it, grinning disarmingly and saying, "All riiiight." He was also the first of the offensive linemen whose contract the club extended before the 2006 season, which, in the absence of redone deals, would have been the last in Cincinnati for all the starting blockers but Braham.

Braham will almost certainly be the first of them replaced, inasmuch as he's the oldest and the Bengals have a couple fine young centers in waiting. But the powers that be have put it off, because they've tried playing without him.

It was Lewis's first game as head coach, the 2003 opener against Denver. The Bengals had released Braham in February and signed him back in April at the NFL minimum wage, figuring he would make an okay backup. The plan was for Mike Goff, a natural guard, to move over to center.

Against Denver, the Cincinnati offense couldn't budge. The next week, Braham was

bent-over and snapping the ball again, and everything was hunky-dory.

At his position, it's not just about blocking, but about recognizing defenses and letting everybody else in on the secrets. "Sometimes," he said, "you come up to the ball and they're in one look, and I get down and they're in a different look. Things happen where (the quarterback) points stuff out, and things happen where I point stuff out. We point all the time. Sometimes it means something, and sometimes it doesn't. That's why we point all the time."

Now and then with mangled fingers, in his case.

Will the co

Rich Braham, the grand old man of the offensive line, was a walk-on at West Virginia where he worked himself up to All-American. That kind of drive is what has made Braham THE UNSUNG HERO OF BENGALDOM. He's played through the darkest days of the franchise, injuries, and the lack of attention centers usually receive. When he retires his attitude should be framed and hung in the locker room as a reminder of how it's done.

Does anybody remember Mel Kiper and the ESPN crew dissing the

Bengals for taking Levi Jones as the 10th overall pick in the 2002

draft? All Levi did was make THE ALL-ROOKIE TEAM, started 59

straight games, and helped the 2005 offense

to a per-game sack average of 1.31,

including no-sack performances

against some of the NFL's top

rushers. So bite me, Mel.

As bad as the Bengals were for all those years, their special teams were worse, ranging week to week from overmatched to comical. When Marvin Lewis took over and declared that special teams were a priority of his, he actually meant it. First, he hired the meticulous Darrin Simmons as special teams coach. Then he drafted players—especially in the lower rounds—with their run-back and coverage skills squarely in mind; also their desire to make the team, because desire—drooling, helmet-smoking ardor—is what special teams are basically about. Then he allotted practice time for the special teams on a regular basis. Then Shayne Graham started making a lot of field goals and Brad St. Louis long-snapped with as much aplomb as a long snapper can muster and Reggie Myles ripped off kamikaze tackles and Peter Warrick beat the Chiefs with a punt return and Tab Perry became a pretty good kickoff returner and the laughs, well, they stopped, because good football is just not that hilarious.

He is the Bengals' right tackle and their right stuff. Marvin Lewis counts on Willie Anderson to keep the other players in the right frame of mind. Carson Palmer counts on him to protect his right side. Anderson himself is preoccupied with the right to play in a Super Bowl someday.

And yet, for his first seven years in Cincinnati—from the time his 340 pounds were drafted in the first round out of Auburn, from Dave Shula to Bruce Coslet to Dick LeBeau—it seemed to Big Willie that everything was going dispiritingly wrong.

In those dismal seasons, the Bengals averaged more than 11 losses. Conventional thinking, however, allowed that few of them had anything to do with the right tackle, and sure enough, the arrival of Lewis proved that popular rationale to be quite correct.

In 2003, Anderson was voted to his first Pro Bowl. In 2004, playing with a banged-up knee that needed surgery, he was voted in again and timbered the way for Rudi Johnson to set a team rushing record. (The conscientious Alabaman had done the same for Corey Dillon in 2000 and 2001.) In 2005, the Fatburger baron completed his third Pro Bowl season, and the sixth in which he hadn't missed a single start in spite of a spate of occupational injuries.

Anderson found, curiously, that as his body aged, the pain somehow became more tolerable, a phenomenon directly attributable to making the playoffs.

"Withou Wil

"Offensive linemen are the

noblest creatures in sports.

YOU'D GO TO WAR WITH THEM,

if not to the prom. Grubbing

around, hands in the dirt, moving

the human pianos arranged against them.

They don't dance or boast or star in commercials.

They're the engine in your decade-old truck, the

potatoes on your plate. They're who you don't miss until

they're gone."—Paul Daugherty

Guard Eric Steinbach is considered the Bengals' most versatile lineman; he has been a guard, a tackle, even a center. He had never played center on *any* level. HOW ABOUT FULLBACK, ERIC? Does anybody remember Pete Johnson?

Everybody watched the 2000 Sugar Bowl, including the Bengals. It was Florida State and Virginia Tech; but really, it was Florida State. It was Peter Warrick, the Seminoles' All-American changer of direction.

He had two touchdowns on pass receptions and another on a punt return, and it was nothing more than what was expected of a player whom nobody could lay a hand on, not even a Southern evangelist.

Nothing less was expected when Cincinnati chose him with the fourth overall pick of the draft. As a Bengal, that was always Warrick's problem. He caught more passes in his first four years than any other player in franchise history, but still, people waited for the mythic Warrick to show up.

And finally, on a November afternoon in 2003, against the undefeated Kansas City Chiefs, he did. He caught six of Jon Kitna's passes for 114 yards, including 77 on a fourth-quarter breakaway touchdown that pretty much did the deed, inasmuch as, a few minutes earlier, he had scorched the Chiefs on a 68-yard punt return for a TD.

"I was trying to bring a little P-Dub back from Florida State," Warrick said.

A year later, his encore season was sabotaged by knee and shin injuries. A year after that, the Bengals released him.

goinggoi

Now you see him...

Now you might not.

Has Been-Gals

Lookin good f

Chris Perry proved his value on third downs, where he was a constant threat. Teamed with Rudi, opposing defenses had their shoulder pads full. Power or speed. Rudi or Chris. Name your poison.

r the ladies.

After his initial season had been completed, people still wondered why the
Bengals had drafted Chris Perry in the
first round. They had Rudi Johnson,
after all, and what to do with another
running back? It became no clearer
when Perry held out and missed nearly
two weeks of training camp, and when
he strained first his hamstring and then
his groin, reducing his rookie year to
two uneventful carries. But 2005 found
him healthy, for the most part, and
worthy of the reputation he had built
up at Michigan. Playing mostly on third
downs, he strutted the kind of can't-
touch-me style that previously had
been the province of Peter Warrick.
While running the ball fetchingly from
scrimmage, Perry also pulled in nearly
as many passes as Warrick did, vacat-
ing the backfield for a nifty 51 catches.
If anyone still has questions concerning Perry's first-round
selection, they may
now be referred
to Carson
Palmer.

10

Ada

Keiwan Ratliff motors around Brett Keisel.

Ratliff wins moment, Steelers win day (October 2005, 27-13).

at the races

Kelley Washington was in his fourth year of minor-league baseball, laboring at third base for the Kane County Cougars of the Florida Marlins farm system, when the bus rolled into South Bend, Ind., one propitious day. Out the window, Washington glimpsed three things: Notre Dame Stadium, another world, and his own future. In fact, once he

enrolled at the University of Tennessee and began to terrorize the Southeastern Conference as a wide receiver, he began to humbly refer to himself as The Future. Two years later, he was a Cincinnati Bengal and, though not frequently enough, performing a somewhat disturbing end zone ritual he called the squirrel dance. "I like the squirrel dance," said receivers coach Hue Jackson, "because when he's doing it, we're scoring touchdowns."

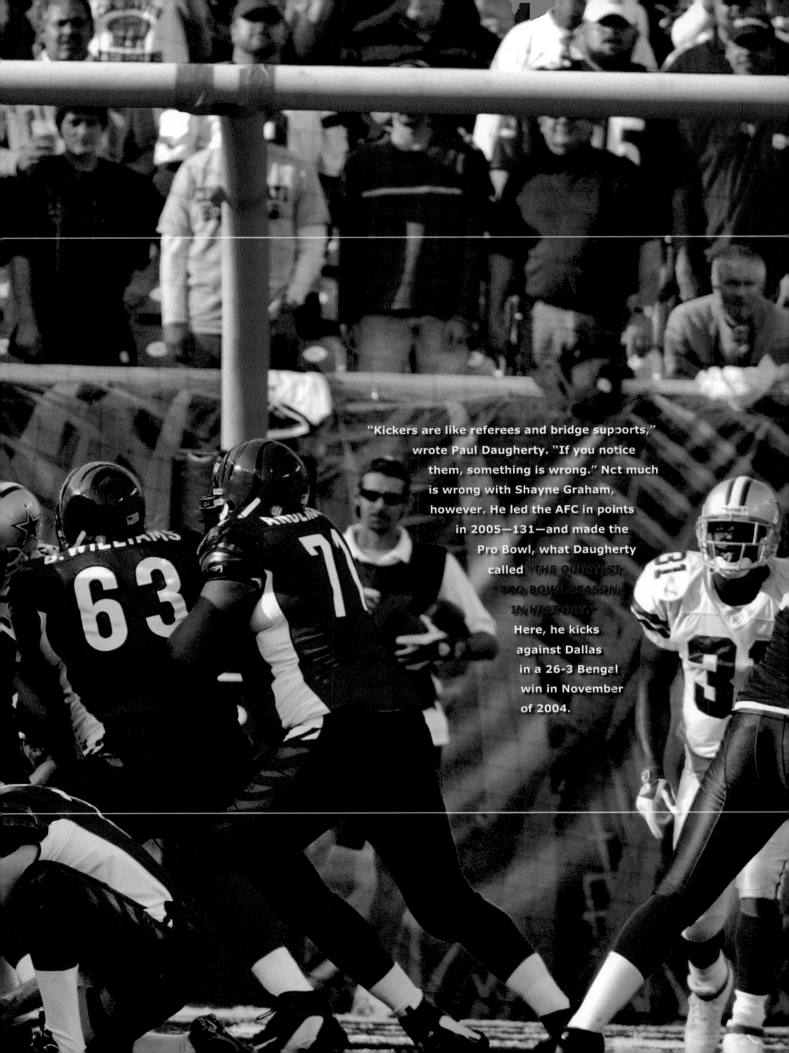

"Kickers are like referees and bridge supports," wrote Paul Daugherty. "If you notice them, something is wrong." Not much is wrong with Shayne Graham, however. He led the AFC in points in 2005—131—and made the Pro Bowl, what Daugherty called "THE QUIETEST PRO BOWL SEASON IN HISTORY." Here, he kicks against Dallas in a 26-3 Bengal win in November of 2004.

Chad and me

There was a time, during his college years, when T. J. Houshmandzadeh thought about taking his mother's last name. Just what the Bengals needed: another Johnson. Actually, Chad Johnson was his roommate on the road back then, when they played for Oregon State. The Beaver with the gold teeth was drafted in the second round. The one with the ponytail was taken in the seventh, 168 players later.

Just as the former came into the NFL with the higher rating and profile, it would seem, judging by the subsequent sound bites and Pro Bowls, that Houshmandzadeh's running mate at wide receiver is the bolder, badder ballplayer.

"Nah," said the one who hasn't led the AFC in catching yardage for three consecutive years. "See, Chad sounds like me.

"Me and Chad, me being better than him and him being better than me, it's just competition. He knows how I feel about his game and how I respect his game, but for me to say, 'Oh, he's better than me . . .' I doubt very seriously that he minds. But if he did, so?"

It's a culture, apparently. While Johnson was acquiring his in South Florida, Houshmandzadeh was carving out something similar in the California town of Barstow, in the middle of the Mojave Desert. That's where Houshmandzadeh —whose father left him to return to Iran around the time T.J. was born—played just a single year of high school football, but did it well enough that he was offered an opportunity at Cerritos Junior College; then at Oregon State; then

in Cincinnati; then, when Peter Warrick was having trouble with his knee, in Cincinnati's starting lineup.

Once there, he would not be dislodged. He caught passes with the same confidence with which he talked about catching passes. Houshmandzadeh's specialty became the difficult reception with defenders waiting to charge him for it. His suspended development, which roughly coincided with Carson Palmer's, completed the Cincinnati passing game. With Johnson out wide and his college teammate posing a comparable threat, the young quarterback was eager to throw to either Beaver.

Or maybe it was Houshmandzadeh out wide and Johnson posing a comparable threat; depending on which one you asked.

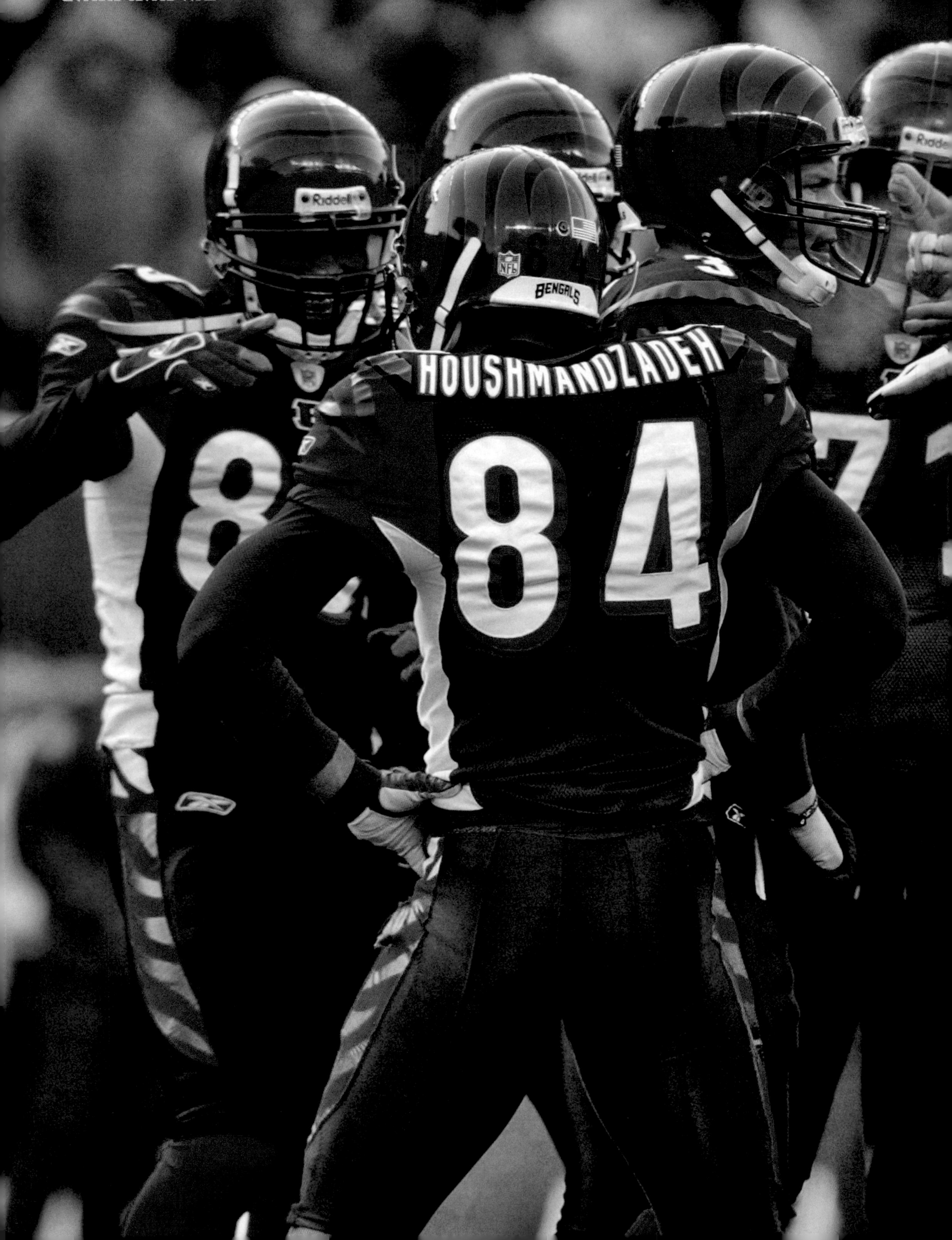
Riddell
BENGALS
HOUSHMANDZADEH
84

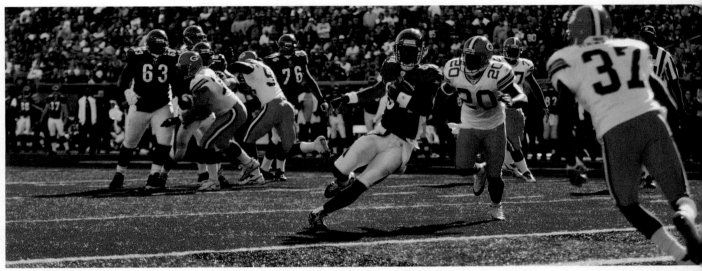

"Suction-cup mitts," they said.

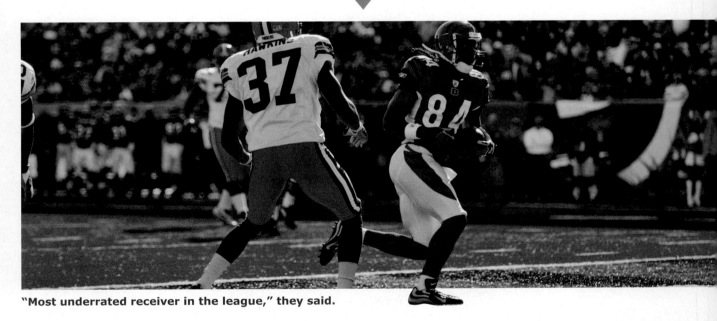

"Most underrated receiver in the league," they said.

114

Struttin his

T.J. Houshmandzadeh was a high school dropout who earned his GED, enrolled in junior college where he helped win two national championships, and ended up as Chad Johnson's teammate at Oregon State. He is of mixed Persian and black ancestry, named after his father, who is Iranian. He took his father's surname instead of his mother's, which is "Johnson." And that, given the number of Johnsons already on the team, is a good thing, or else we might have a team called THE CINCINNATI JOHNSONS.

▼

STUFF

Once a rivalry

The 2005 season, and in particular the agonizing way it ended for Carson Palmer and the Bengals, represented a significant shift for the Cincinnati franchise. Its steamiest rival, and the team with which it was necessarily most concerned, became the Pittsburgh Steelers.

To some, however—and their number includes all members of the Brown family but most notably Mike—the best Sundays will always be the ones in which the Bengals have taken care of Cleveland. Sixty years of history, and more than forty of hard feelings, are not easily set aside.

Bengals owner Mike Brown, of course, is the son of Paul, who founded the Cleveland organization and lent it a name. The Browns first competed in the All-American Football Conference, which lasted four years, which was long enough for Cleveland to win four championships. Dealing from strength, the Browns then joined up with the NFL and successfully transferred their excellence, winning the league title in their first go-around (1950) and then twice more in their first six seasons, each of which found them in the championship game. All of that is by way of saying that Paul Brown's team was getting along quite well before Art Modell used borrowed money to shoulder his way into ownership, whereupon he grabbed Brown's office for himself. Two years later, he fired the man who literally symbolized the franchise.

Brown's response was to found and coach the Bengals, setting up perhaps the most personal rivalry in professional sport. The only thing it lacked, for the most part, was two good teams, which often led, in turn, to a ferocious need to be better than the other, at least.

In that context, losing the first game ever played at Paul Brown Stadium wouldn't have been so regrettable for the Bengals had not the opponent been a bad Browns team. Losing the last game of the 2003 season, with the playoffs perhaps on the line, wouldn't have been so disgraceful had not the opponent been another bad Browns team.

After two Cincinnati victories in 2005, the tally stood at 33-32, Cleveland, with diminishing fervor. The rivalry had been seriously compromised when, in 1996, Modell stole his team—others thought of it as Cleveland's, actually—out of Ohio, establishing the Baltimore Ravens. With them, and with Marvin Lewis as defensive coordinator, he finally won a Super Bowl. Within three years of that, he had taken his money and retired, beating the Bengals in his final game.

What it all means is that Cincinnati's three opponents in the AFC North—Pittsburgh, Baltimore and the second coming of the Browns —may all be considered archrivals of one fashion or another. Cleveland is just a little more arch than the others, and will remain so until the Bengals are bought by somebody named Steeler.

The Georgia boys did okay in the 2005 opener at Cleveland. It was Cincinnati's first road win in ten years, and David Pollack (99) had six tackles, one behind his old teammate, Odell Thurman. Thurman had an interception, though, so at the end of the day, Pollack was in arrears.

"Crash From Past: Bengals Are Out," read the headlines,

after the Browns eliminated the Bengals from the playoffs in 2003.

"CHAD JOHNSON HAD NOTHING TO CELEBRATE," said the AP story.

"The Bengals missed out on the long-awaited winning record.

One last time: Can you say Bungles?" Well, you could.

But not for long. For the Bengals would soon be

playing the kind of defense seen here, with

Brian Simmons (56), Mark Roman (20),

and Kevin Kaesviharn (34).

But on this one afternoon,

when the Browns prevailed,

22-14, there wasn't quite

enough of it.

119

Kevin Walter's finest Bengal moment
came in this 2005 opener against Cleveland
when he scored on a 20-yard pass from Carson
Palmer. Walter, a receiver and solid special
teamer, would go to Houston in 2006, undone
by the numbers game.

Cornerback Kelvan Ratliff got the monkey off his back: his first NFL interception. It kept the Browns out of the end zone in the second half of the 2003 overtime. He also had six tackles and a fumble recovery. Ratliff was a Columbus, Ohio, All-American who somehow missed Ohio State and ended up at Florida. There, he was the first player in almost half a century to start at both cornerback and wide receiver, traits that made him another fan favorite in Bengaldom.

The defense had a new look in 2005 when the Bengals opened

in hostile territory—Cleveland—and Tory James covered rookie hotshot,

Braylon Edwards. Edwards, the nation's top receiver in 2004 (he held

the Big Ten mark for touchdowns with 39), is introduced to the NFL

by Tory's embrace, which said, "Welcome to JetBlack&Blue.

WE EXPECT A LITTLE TURBULENCE TODAY, especially

in the Red Zone. Please buckle up."

The trenches

In Marvin Lewis's first draft as a head coach, the Bengals didn't select a single defensive player who was still among them three years later. They made up for it the next year, taking six in a row after Chris Perry. In 2005, the team's top two choices were linebackers from Georgia.

Lewis might be excused for thinking in the beginning—if indeed he did—that he could make a great defense out of whatever Cincinnati presented him. As defensive coordinator in Baltimore, he had gathered, crafted, and coached-up a unit that set records while winning the Super Bowl. It was taken for granted—by everyone else, if not him—that the new Bengals would forge their identity without the football.

In retrospect, the plight of Lewis's predecessor, Dick LeBeau, might have been taken into account. With the Pittsburgh Steelers, LeBeau, too, had been one of the game's most innovative and respected defensive coordinators. As a head coach in Cincinnati, however, that simply didn't translate. Shortly after LeBeau returned to his old job in Pittsburgh, the Steelers won a Super Bowl.

Perhaps, then, the difficulty could be traced to the fact that, with the exception of Justin Smith in 2001, the Bengals went 11 years without drafting a defensive lineman in the first three rounds.

Nor have they ever—*ever*—taken a true cornerback in the first round. Their principal problem, though, had become stopping the run, and the dearth of highly rated defensive linemen might have had a little something to do with that.

The trouble persisted under Lewis, which is why he kept looking to free agency for big guys to blunt the ground game. Over the years, the Bengals had pursued such hulking luminaries as Sam Adams, Warren Sapp, Daryl Gardener and Corey Simon for that purpose. Before the 2005 season, they did latch onto Bryan Robinson, a helpful tackle whose profile was a little lower than the fellows above. Then, before the 2006 season, they made another advance on Adams, this time succeeding.

They also signed a safety, Dexter Jackson, who came with strong run-stopping credentials. The other starting safety, Madieu Williams, had been injured for most of the 2005 season. In the opinion of more than a few, Williams was Cincinnati's best defensive player, the keystone of the 2004 draft class that produced two additional starters in Landon Johnson and Robert Geathers. With Keiwan Ratliff and Caleb Miller also arriving in that group, and David Pollack and Odell Thurman topping the 2005 draft list, Cincinnati's defense had become dependent upon—and promising due to—a broad, swift nucleus of young players.

Not meeting that description, however, were veteran Pro Bowl cornerbacks Tory James and Deltha O'Neal, whose ball-sensing had facilitated a battery of interceptions early in the 2005 season. In terms of yardage and league rankings, the Bengals' defense did not statistically improve much in 2005. It did, however, play its part in the trek to the playoffs.

Its spiritual leader was linebacker Brian Simmons, who, like former running mate Takeo Spikes, had been a first-round draft choice in 1998. Seldom spectacular, Simmons was, however, a player without a discernible weakness. "He's strong," observed one-time teammate Kevin Hardy of the handsome tackler. "He's Mandingo."

Even so, the Cincinnati defense struggled to play strong as a unit. Lewis had hired Leslie Frazier as his first defensive coordinator, but their philosophies collided and after two seasons Frazier was replaced by Chuck Bresnahan. The charge was to simplify. And stop the run.

"We had a saying in Baltimore," related Lewis, "that they've got a West Coast offense, but we've got an East Coast defense. I think that's what has been established here."

That, at least, was what was being established in Cincinnati. It was just taking a while, is all.

The concept of the weight room was
well-established before Justin Smith arrived
in Cincinnati in 2001 as a first-round draft choice
out of Missouri. Rarely, however, had it played
such a part in the development of a defensive
end. Without lifting, Smith was just a big
ol' country boy; and frankly, not all that
big. With it, he became an immediate
starter in the NFL, and his 8.5 sacks
the first time around were the most
ever by a Bengals rookie.

Deltha O'Neal helped launch the 2005 season when he robbed Daunte Culpepper blind in the Bengals' second game, picking off the Viking quarterback three times. O'Neal defensed a pass that led to a Kevin Kaesviharn interception, and led the Bengals in total tackles (8). It wasn't a bad day's work, which was an apt description of the day in April, 2004, when the Bengals acquired the disgruntled Pro

Bowler from Denver. Remember 2004? The Bengals beat Denver at home, 23-10, and on his second return of the game, O'Neal zigzagged 17 yards to the Denver 45 where he went out of bounds—and directly into his old coach, Mike Shanahan. Next, he intercepted Jake Plummer. Injury to insult. Then he celebrated. "I had to, man," he said. "I just wanted Mike to see that, since I know he don't like it."

"That

In 1998 the Bengals selected two linebackers—Takeo Spikes and Brian Simmons—
in the first round of the draft. Spikes was the more chiseled and vocal, and consequently
celebrated. But when, upon the arrival of Marvin Lewis, he chiseled and vocalized his way
out of town, it was Simmons who became the veteran leader of the Cincinnati defense.
Early in that 2003 season, he grappled the ball away from the Baltimore quarterback, and
then kept doing things like that. By 2005, finally—and by virtue of a snatch-happy,
Simmons-style defense—the Bengals managed a swift beginning to a winning season.

This is the day after Christmas, 2004. The Giants led 22-17 when Keiwan Ratliff waited under a New York punt with just over two minutes to play. The punt was 43 yards. Ratliff's return was 42, and the Bengals were on New York's 23-yard line. Kitna threw three uncatchable passes and on 4th down, he floated up another—slightly catchable, thanks to T.J. Houshmandzadeh on the other end. Two plays later, Chad Johnson scored the winning TD. Said tackle Carl Powell, "I think the football gods looked down on us today."

Smith's 34 sacks rank fifth all time among
Bengals—one-half sack behind Tim Krumrie.

A triumvirate of defensive stalwarts here, ranging from Justin Smith (left)

to John Thorton (97), who holds the serendipitous distinction of being the

last Bengal to block an opponent's field goal as well as being the last opponent

to block a Bengals' field goal try. Says something about being in the right place.

Then there's Robert Geathers (91), who forced a Hines Ward fumble in the crucial

December 4, 2005, Pitttsburgh game and helped stop a scoring threat. Geathers

saw himself as a pro footballer ever

since he saw his uncle, Jumpy

Geathers, a good pro lineman,

shove a blocker into his own

quarterback, a technique

he called "the forklift."

They were some sixty-odd thousand of America's most indomitable sports fans, banding stoutly together for over a decade until the 2004 team beat New York and Philadelphia and finished 8-8. They were such a famously hardy group that over 400 of them came out on Christmas Day and shoveled snow at Paul Brown Stadium for $8 an hour. Said Marvin Lewis in thanking them, "They obviously know what we mean when we tell the players how important it is to 'keep on shoveling.'"

He was an old man when he arrived in Cincinnati in 2003, because each year at linebacker in the NFL is a dog's year, and Kevin Hardy already had seven of them. He'd won the Dick Butkus Award as an Illinois senior, in addition to being a consensus All-American. Then he was the first defensive player taken in the 1996 draft, and played six good years with Jacksonville, where he was All-Pro. He came to town as a free agent, a solid team guy who held the fort until the young guys—Thurman and Pollack—arrived. An old man at, what? Thirty-two? Who, other than a linebacker, is old at 32? Is there life after linebacker?

the trenches

When Landon Johnson was at Purdue he won the team's Pit Bull Award, given to Purdue's most intense player. "**THE SILENT ASSASSIN**," they called him, and in two consecutive seasons he forced seven players out of the game following his ferocious hits. If they hadn't given him the Pit Bull Award, he would have *taken* it.

▶

▲

Kevin Kaesviharn came out of Augustana College and played Arena Football with the Iowa Barnstormers, worked off-season as a substitute teacher, did a stint with the XFL, and—finally in 2001—became a Bengal. At heart, he's still a teacher, though. Here, he's taking Keyshawn Johnson to school.

141